SIDEWAYS ARITHMETIC FROM

WAYSIDE SCHOOL

LOUIS SACHAR

MORE SIDEWAYS ARITHMETIC FROM WAYSIDE SCHOOL

MULTIPLICATION

Illustrated by Peter Allen

BLOOMSBURY
CHILDREN'S
BOOKS

First published in Great Britain in 2004 by Bloomsbury Publishing Plc
38 Soho Square, London, W1D 3HB

First published in the U.S. by Scholastic Inc.

Text copyright © Louis Sachar 1989
Illustrations copyright © Peter Allen 2004
The moral rights of the author and illustrator have been asserted

A CIP catalogue record of this book is available from the British Library

ISBN 0 7475 6913 4

Typeset by Tracey Cunnell

Printed in Great Britain by Clays Ltd, St Ives plc

10 9 8 7 6 5 4 3 2 1

All papers used by Bloomsbury Publishing are natural,
recyclable products made from wood grown in well-managed forests.
The manufacturing processes conform to the environmental
regulations of the country of origin.

TO MY MOTHER

CONTENTS

SPLAT

"HUH?"

THAT IS THE REACTION I HAVE HEARD MOST OFTEN FROM KIDS WHO HAVE READ 'SIDEWAYS ARITHMETIC FROM WAYSIDE SCHOOL'.

I'VE ALSO GOTTEN LOTS OF LETTERS FROM KIDS WHO SAY THINGS LIKE,

> "DEAR MR. SACHAR,
> I LIKED YOUR BOOK 'SIDEWAYS ARITHMETIC FROM WAYSIDE SCHOOL', BUT I DON'T UNDERSTAND THE PROBLEMS."

NOW I DON'T UNDERSTAND HOW KIDS CAN LIKE THE BOOK IF THEY DON'T UNDERSTAND THE PROBLEMS. MAYBE THEY'RE JUST BEING POLITE.

BUT IT'S NOT JUST KIDS. TEACHERS HAVE ALSO CONFIDED IN ME THAT THEY DIDN'T UNDERSTAND THE BOOK.

SO YOU MAY BE WONDERING WHY I HAVE WRITTEN THIS SEQUEL. IT IS BECAUSE I THINK THE PROBLEMS ARE A LOT OF FUN. THEY WERE FUN FOR ME TO MAKE UP, AND THEY ARE FUN TO SOLVE — ONCE YOU GET THE HANG OF IT.

YES, THE PROBLEMS ARE HARD. YOU HAVE TO THINK. YOU CAN'T JUST READ QUICKLY THROUGH IT, LIKE THE OTHER WAYSIDE SCHOOL BOOKS.

YOU MAY WANT TO ASK A PARENT OR TEACHER TO
HELP YOU GET STARTED, ALTHOUGH LIKE I SAID,
MANY ADULTS WILL HAVE TROUBLE, TOO. ACTUALLY I
THINK THIS WOULD BE A GREAT BOOK FOR A PARENT
AND CHILD TO FIGURE OUT TOGETHER. THE PARENT
COULD HELP THE CHILD, AND VICE-VERSA.
YOU DO NOT NEED TO READ 'SIDEWAYS ARITHMETIC
FROM WAYSIDE SCHOOL' FIRST. SOME OF THE
PROBLEMS IN THAT BOOK ARE HARDER THAN THE
PROBLEMS IN THIS BOOK. SOME MAY BE EASIER.
I ORGANIZED THIS BOOK A LITTLE DIFFERENTLY, AND
I THINK THAT SHOULD HELP. AT THE BACK OF THE
BOOK, THERE ARE 'CLUES', 'HINTS' AND FINALLY, 'ANSWERS'.
THE 'CLUES' TELL YOU HOW TO BEGIN TO TRY TO SOLVE
EACH PROBLEM. THAT IS VERY IMPORTANT. PROBABLY
THE HARDEST PART OF EACH PROBLEM IS JUST TRYING
TO FIGURE OUT WHERE TO BEGIN. ONCE YOU FIGURE
OUT HOW TO GET STARTED, THE REST OF THE
PROBLEM IS MUCH EASIER.
A 'HINT' WILL GIVE YOU PART OF THE ANSWER.
AND THE 'ANSWER' WILL TELL YOU THE ANSWER.
(DUH!)

Louis Sachar

WHY BOYS AND GIRLS ARE SILLY

Allison's birthday was next Saturday. She brought birthday party invitations to class. She invited every girl in Mrs. Jewls's class, but only two boys, Jason and Stephen.

Jason wasn't sure he wanted to go. "Why don't you invite some more boys?" he said.

"I can't," said Allison. "Two are okay. But if more than two boys come, then all the boys start acting real silly."

"That's right," said Rondi. "Two's the limit, when it comes to boys."

"That's ridiculous," said Jason.

"I'm insulted," said Stephen.

"It's true," said Allison.

Just then Joe and John came over. "What's going on?" asked John.

"Allison says if more than two boys get together, we all act real silly," said Stephen.

"That's dumb!" said John, pounding his fist on a desk. "Ouch!" he exclaimed, and shook his hand in the air.

"Hey, I'm not silly!" said Jason. He stuck out his tongue and jumped up and down.

"It's redickle-dockle!" agreed Joe.

Stephen raised his arms in the air and made monkey noises.

"Settle down!" called Mrs. Jewls. "What's the matter with you children?"

"Allison invited Stephen and me to her birthday party," complained Jason.

"That's good, isn't it?" asked Mrs. Jewls.

"We're the only boys," said Stephen. "She says if she invites more boys, then all the boys will act silly."

"She's right," said Mrs. Jewls. "It's a matter of simple arithmetic." She picked up a piece of chalk and wrote the equation on the board.

PROBLEM 1

$$
\begin{array}{r}
\text{boys} \\
+\ \text{boys} \\
\hline
\text{silly}
\end{array}
$$

s = ? o = ? i = ? l = ? b = ? y = ?

Jason studied the board. "I guess we are silly," he said. "Arithmetic doesn't lie."

(Looking at the problem, each letter stands for a single digit number (a number between zero and nine). All the **s**'s are the same number. All the **b**'s are the same number, but different from **s**. And so forth. You have to figure out what number each letter represents, so that it all adds up correctly.

If you need help a **clue** can be found on page 88. If you still need help after that, a **hint** can be found on page 102.)

All the girls were very excited. They danced around the room singing, "Boys and boys are silly! Boys and boys are silly! Boys and boys are silly!"

"Girls and girls are silly, too," said Mrs. Jewls.

The girls stopped singing.

Mrs. Jewls put it on the board.

PROBLEM 2

$$
\begin{array}{r}
\text{girls} \\
+\ \text{girls} \\
\hline
\text{silly}
\end{array}
$$

s = ? l = ? y = ? r = ? i = ? g = ?

The girls yelled and screamed, and made faces, and once again proved that arithmetic doesn't lie.

(You need to forget about the first problem in solving this one. In other words, **s** may stand for a different number in this problem than it did in the last problem.

A **clue** is on page 89. A **hint** is on page 102.)

CHAPTER 2

SOME CRASS WORDS ABOUT WOMEN'S UNDERWEAR

"What are arcs and bras?" asked Mrs. Jewls.
Dana gasped. "A teacher shouldn't talk about
bras!" she said.

"Why not?" asked Mrs. Jewls.

"It's crass," said Rondi.

"You're right!" said Mrs. Jewls.
She put it on the board.

PROBLEM 3

$$\begin{array}{r} \textbf{arcs} \\ + \ \textbf{bras} \\ \hline \textbf{crass} \end{array}$$

c = ?   r = ?   a = ?   b = ?   s = ?

(**Clue** on page 89. **Hint** on page 102.)

Mrs. Jewls put the following problems on the board. Can you solve them?

PROBLEM 4

$$\begin{array}{r} \textbf{llama} \\ - \ \textbf{seal} \\ \hline \textbf{seal} \end{array}$$

m = ?   e = ?   a = ?   l = ?   s = ?

(**Clue** on page 89. **Hint** on page 102.)

PROBLEM 5

$$\begin{array}{r} l\,i\,p \\ +\ \ l\,i\,t \\ \hline p\,i\,p\,e \end{array}$$

t = ?   e = ?   p = ?   i = ?   l = ?

(**Clue** on page 90. **Hint** on page 102.)

PROBLEM 6

$$\begin{array}{r} p\,e\,p \\ +\ \ p\,e\,n \\ \hline e\,r\,n\,e \end{array}$$

p = ?   e = ?   n = ?   r = ?

(**Clue** on page 90. **Hint** on page 102.)

(The problems will now get a little bit harder... .)

CHAPTER 3

SUE'S NEW DOG

Sue got a new dog.

"His name is Fangs," said Sue. "He has big teeth."

"Ooh, he sounds like a mean dog," said Calvin.

"No, he's a good dog," said Sue.

"He sounds mean," Calvin maintained.

"Let's ask Mrs. Jewls," said Sue. "She knows everything."

They presented the problem to their teacher. Mrs. Jewls put it on the board.

PROBLEM 7

$$\begin{array}{r} good \\ + \quad dog \\ \hline fangs \end{array}$$

d = ?   o = ?   g = ?   f = ?
a = ?   n = ?   s = ?

"Fangs is a good dog," Mrs. Jewls concluded.

(**Clue** on page 90. **Hint** on page 102.)

19

FOUR TIMES TOO

"It's too hot!" Myron complained as he wiped his face with his sleeve.

"It's too too hot," said Dameon.

"It's too too too hot," said D.J.

"It's too too too too hot," said Joy.

"You're right," said Mrs. Jewls.

PROBLEM 8

```
  too
  too
  too
+ too
─────
  hot
```

h = ?   o = ?   t = ?

(**Clue** on page 91. **Hint** on page 102.)

Mrs. Jewls put the following problems on the board. Can you solve them?

PROBLEM 9

$$\begin{array}{r} \text{her} \\ + \ \text{hurl} \\ \hline \text{sells} \end{array}$$

l = ? u = ? s = ? h = ? e = ? r = ?

(**Clue** on page 91. **Hint** on page 102.)

PROBLEM 10

$$\begin{array}{r} \text{spit} \\ + \ \text{sip} \\ \hline \text{tips} \end{array}$$

s = ?   p = ?   i = ?   t = ?

(**Clue** on page 91. **Hint** on page 102.)

PROBLEM 11

$$
\begin{array}{r}
\text{pet} \\
\text{pet} \\
+\ \text{pet} \\
\hline
\text{tape}
\end{array}
$$

t = ?   **a = ?**   **p = ?**   **e = ?**

(**Clue** on page 92. **Hint** on page 102.)

PROBLEM 12

$$
\begin{array}{r}
\text{yea} \\
+\ \text{yay} \\
\hline
\text{aye}
\end{array}
$$

a = ?   **y = ?**   **e = ?**

(**Clue** on page 92. **Hint** on page 102.)

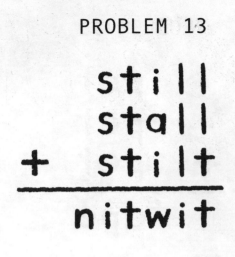

$$\begin{array}{r} \text{still} \\ \text{stall} \\ + \text{stilt} \\ \hline \text{nitwit} \end{array}$$

w = ?   i = ?   n = ?   l = ?
a = ?   s = ?   t = ?

(**Clue** on page 92. **Hint** on page 102.)

(The problems will now get a little bit harder... .)

CHAPTER 5

MiSS WORM

Miss Worm taught the class in the room just below Mrs. Jewls's class. She was often disturbed by the strange noises that came from above.

One day she came up to complain. "Why are you so noisy?" she asked.

"We're doing arithmetic," explained Mrs. Jewls.

"When my class does arithmetic, we work quietly," said Miss Worm.

"It always gets us very excited," said Mrs. Jewls.

Miss Worm couldn't imagine how arithmetic could be exciting, so she asked if she could watch. "Add something," she said.

"Like what?" asked Mrs. Jewls.

"Eight plus eight," suggested Miss Worm.

So everybody in the class tried to add eight plus eight.

"I know it ends in two," said Stephen.

"No, it doesn't," said Miss Worm.

"Yes, it does," said Mrs. Jewls, who thought Stephen had said it ended in "top." But either way, Stephen was right.

Mrs. Jewls put the problem on the board.

PROBLEM 14

$$\begin{array}{r} \mathrm{eight} \\ + \ \mathrm{eight} \\ \hline \mathrm{tattoo} \end{array}$$

"Wait a minute! Wait a minute!" shouted Miss Worm. "I didn't mean the word **eight**. I meant the number, **8**."

"But Miss Worm," said Mrs. Jewls. "There isn't an **8** anywhere in the problem."

a = ?   h = ?   o = ?   g = ?
t = ?   i = ?   e = ?

(And remember, there isn't an eight anywhere in the problem!)

(**Clue** on page 93. **Hint** on page 102.)

Miss Worm tried to get the class to add one plus one, and two plus two, but without any better results.

PROBLEM 15

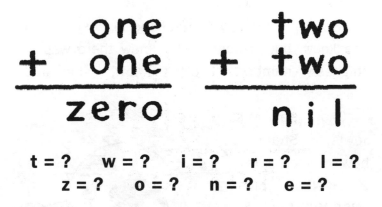

```
   one          two
+  one       +  two
_____     _____
  zero          nil
```

t = ?   w = ?   i = ?   r = ?   l = ?
z = ?   o = ?   n = ?   e = ?

(These two problems have to be solved together. So, for example, whatever the letter **o** is in the first problem, it has to be the same in the second.)

(**Clue** on page 93. **Hint** on page 102.)

Sharie fell asleep in class.

"Excuse me, Mrs. Jewls," said Miss Worm. "But one of your students is asleep."

"Yes, that's Sharie," said Mrs. Jewls. "She's my best student."

"But she's sleeping!" said Miss Worm.

"I know," said Mrs. Jewls. "Sharie learns best when she's asleep."

Sharie started to snore. "Zzzz... ."

"Now she's snoring!" said Miss Worm.

"She's very smart," Mrs. Jewls agreed. "Ask her any problem. She'll know the answer. What's the biggest number you know?"

Miss Worm tried to think of the biggest number she knew, but of course she knew there was no "biggest" number. "I don't know," she said. "Zillions!"

"Okay," said Mrs. Jewls. "Sharie, how much is **ZILLIONS** plus **MISS WORM**?

"ZZZZZZZZZ," snored Sharie.

"See," Mrs. Jewls said proudly. "I told you she was smart."

M I S S W O R M
+ Z I L L I O N S

Z Z Z Z Z Z Z Z Z

Wait! Stop! Don't try to solve the problem yet! There's more.

As an author, I always try to be fair. Well, I just realized I haven't been fair to the letter **Q**. Nowhere in this book, nor in *Sideways Arithmetic From Wayside School*, was there a problem with the letter **Q** in it. So, in the interest of fairness I want you to solve for **Q** in this problem, even though it's not there. If it was there, what would it be?

I'll tell you this much. **Q** is a larger number than **N**. Okay, now you can go ahead and solve the problem.

S = ?   W = ?   I = ?   R = ?   L = ?
O = ?   N = ?   M = ?   Z = ?   Q = ?

(**Clue** on page 93. **Hint** on page 102.)

CHAPTER 6

MiSS WORM FiNALLY UNDERSTANDS!

Speaking of tattoos, Calvin had a tattoo, just above his foot. The following passage can be found on page 88 of *Wayside School Is Falling Down*.

"You're so lucky, Calvin," said Rondi. "I wish I could get a tattoo too! Instead I got a tutu."

"I got a tutu too," said Dana.

Mrs. Jewls pointed to Calvin's tattoo, and asked, "How much is **his foot** plus **tutu too**?"

hisfoot
+ tututoo

Miss Worm looked at the problem and frowned. She threw up her hands in disgust. "Who knows!" she said, and started toward the door.

"Don't tell them the answer," said Mrs. Jewls. She sighed and put the next problem on the board. "How much is **peppers** plus **pig lips**?" she asked.

peppers
+ piglips

"I give up!" shouted Miss Worm. She stormed out of the room, slamming the door behind her.

"Miss Worm is very good at adding in her head," said Mrs. Jewls. "But I wish she wouldn't give away the answers."

$$\begin{array}{r} \text{hisfoot} \\ +\ \text{tututoo} \\ \hline \text{whoknows} \end{array}$$

f = ?   i = ?   s = ?   h = ?   n = ?
u = ?   t = ?   w = ?   o = ?   k = ?

(**Clue** on page 94. **Hint** on page 102.)

PROBLEM 18

peppers
+ piglips
igiveup

s = ?   i = ?   l = ?   v = ?   e = ?
r = ?   p = ?   u = ?   g = ?

(**Clue** on page 94. **Hint** on page 102.)

(Coming up next will be the hardest problem in the book... .)

33

tHE QUiz tHAT WOULDN'T POP

(Like I said, this next problem, **Problem 19**, will be the hardest problem in the book. But I don't even know what the problem is yet. Let me explain. Mrs. Jewls is planning to give her class a test next week. For the nineteenth problem in this book, I will choose the hardest question from that test.)

PROBLEM 19

"We will have a pop quiz sometime next week," Mrs. Jewls told her class on Friday afternoon.
Everybody groaned.

"What day will it be?" asked Jenny.

"I'm not going to tell you," said Mrs. Jewls. "That's why it's called a 'pop quiz.' You won't know when it's going to pop. It will be one day next week, but I won't tell you which day."

"Hey, that's not fair!" said Jason. "That means I have to study all weekend, and the test might not be until next Friday!"

"That's right," said Mrs. Jewls.

Everybody groaned.

"That means we have to worry all week," griped Joy.

"Can you give us a hint?" asked Paul. "Will it be Monday? Just let us know if it's going to be Monday, so I know whether to study this weekend."

"No hints," said Mrs. Jewls. "It will be a total surprise. We will have the quiz first thing in the morning. But you won't know which morning until I say, 'Take out your pencil and paper for the pop quiz.' "

Everybody grumbled and groaned.

"I think surprises are fun," said Mrs. Jewls.

No one else did.

Suddenly Todd's eyes lit up. He smiled. "Hold on!" he said. "I just thought of something. It can't be Friday!"

"What are you talking about?" said Mrs. Jewls.

"You said it will be a surprise, right?" asked Todd.

"Yes," said Mrs. Jewls.

"Well then," Todd concluded. "If we haven't had the test on Monday, Tuesday, Wednesday, or Thursday, then on Friday we'll know it's coming. So it won't be a surprise!"

Mrs. Jewls thought it over. "I guess you're right, Todd," she agreed. "Okay, the quiz won't be on Friday."

"Way to go, Todd!" cheered Mac.

Everyone thanked Todd.

Except Joy. "Big deal!" she griped. "So it won't be on Friday. It still could be on Monday, Tuesday, Wednesday or Thursday."

"It can't be Thursday!" Bebe exclaimed with delight.

"What do you mean?" asked Mrs. Jewls.

"Well, we know it won't be on Friday," said Bebe. "So if the quiz hasn't popped on Monday, Tuesday, or Wednesday, we'll know it's going to pop on Thursday. And so then it won't be a surprise anymore."

Mrs. Jewls scratched her head. "You're right, Bebe," she conceded. "The quiz can't be on Thursday. But that still leaves Monday, Tuesday or Wednesday, so you better all study hard this weekend because—"

"It can't be Wednesday," interrupted Maurecia. "Because if it hasn't popped by Tuesday, we'll know it has to be Wednesday. And then it won't be a surprise!"

"Wait a second," said Mrs. Jewls. "Let me think about this." She rubbed her face. "It can't be Friday," she muttered, "so then it can't be Thursday... ." She rubbed her face harder. "It's no good if it's not a surprise. You're right, Maurecia! Okay, so the quiz will be on Monday or Tuesday. But I still won't tell you which day. You won't know until I say, 'Take out your pencil and paper for the—' "

"IT CAN'T BE TUESDAY!" Benjamin, Leslie, and Stephen shouted together.

"If we don't have it on Monday ..." said Benjamin.

"... then we'll know it's coming on Tuesday ..." said Leslie.

"... and it won't be a surprise!" said Stephen.

Mrs. Jewls frowned. "All right then, it will be Monday, but you won't know until — of course you'll know. I just told you it was Monday!" She shook her head. "Let's just forget the whole thing. There will be no pop quiz."

Everybody cheered.

(So, Mrs. Jewls never gave the quiz. There is no **Problem 19**. Sorry.)

CHAPTER 8

OH, NO!

"It's time for multiplication," said Mrs. Jewls.

"Oh no!" shouted Deedee.

"I don't get it," complained Todd.

"Today is not my day," said Benjamin. "I am going to move away."

"Don't worry, hon'," said Mrs. Jewls. "We'll start with those."

PROBLEM 20

```
      my
  X   am
  _____
     day
     my
  _____
    away
```

m = ?   y = ?   w = ?   a = ?   d = ?

(**Clue** on page 95. **Hint** on page 102.)

PROBLEM 21

```
      oh
  X   no
  _____
    zoo
   hon
  _____
   hero
```

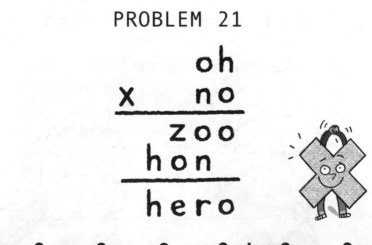

z = ?   e = ?   n = ?   r = ?   h = ?   o = ?

(**Clue** on page 95. **Hint** on page 102.)

PROBLEM 22

$$
\begin{array}{r}
\text{get} \\
\times \quad \text{it} \\
\hline
\text{her} \\
\text{nine} \\
\hline
\text{nicer}
\end{array}
$$

r = ?   i = ?   c = ?   h = ?

g = ?   e = ?   n = ?   t = ?

(**Clue** on page 95. **Hint** on page 102.)

PROBLEM 23

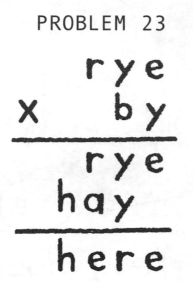

```
    r y e
x     b y
---------
    r y e
  h a y
---------
  h e r e
```

h = ? e = ? a = ? r = ? b = ? y = ?

(**Clue** on page 96. **Hint** on page 102.)

(The problems will now get a little bit harder... .)

CHAPter 9

FOREIGN LANGUAGE LESSON

Mrs. Jewls taught the class how to say "yes" in three different languages.

Yes in Spanish is *sí*, which is pronounced like "see."

Yes in French is *oui*, which is pronounced like "we."

Yes in Russian is *da*, which is pronounced like "da."

"Does everybody understand?" she asked.

"We," said Joe.

"See," said Jason.

"Duh," said Jenny.

"No, *da*," said Mrs. Jewls. "Now I want everyone to write 'yes' in another language, and use it in a multiplication problem."

PROBLEM 24

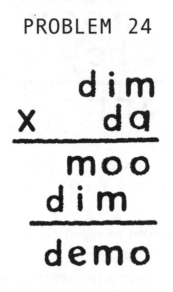

```
        d i m
 X       d a
    ─────────
      m o o
    d i m
    ─────────
    d e m o
```

i = ? d = ? e = ? a = ? m = ? o = ?

(**Clue** on page 96. **Hint** on page 103.)

PROBLEM 25

$$\begin{array}{r} say \\ \times \quad si \\ \hline nosy \\ icy \quad \\ \hline annoy \end{array}$$

s = ?   a = ?   y = ?   c = ?
o = ?   i = ?   n = ?

(**Clue** on page 96. **Hint** on page 103.)

PROBLEM 26

```
     r o t
x      a t
———————————
   r u d e
 o u i
———————————
 e e r i e
```

i = ?   d = ?   e = ?   a = ?
t = ?   o = ?   u = ?   r = ?

(**Clue** on page 97. **Hint** on page 103.)

(The problems will now get a little harder... .)

CHAPTER 10

HE, SHE, WE, AND EWE

PROBLEM 27

$$
\begin{array}{r}
\text{she} \\
\times\ \text{he} \\
\hline
\text{yes} \\
\text{she} \\
\hline
\text{sass}
\end{array}
$$

h = ?   a = ?   y = ?   e = ?   s = ?

(**Clue** on page 97. **Hint** on page 103.)

PROBLEM 28

```
        ewe
x        he
      ─────
       yay
      sash
      ─────
     sissy
```

a = ? y = ? e = ? w = ? i = ? s = ? h = ?

(**Clue** on page 97. **Hint** on page 103.)

PROBLEM 29

```
        aid
x        we
      ─────
       lied
      lewd
      ─────
      added
```

w = ? a = ? i = ? l = ? e = ? d = ?

(**Clue** on page 98. **Hint** on page 103.)

CHAPTER 11

REPORT CARDS

Once again, it was time for Mrs. Jewls to write report cards. It was a job she hated. Instead of giving out grades, she would rather give out hugs.

But at least this time it would be done by computer. She had bought herself a home computer, and throughout the year whenever she graded a test or checked a child's homework, she entered the results in the computer.

Now all she had to do was run the program, and the computer would instantly print out twenty-nine report cards, complete with teacher's comments.

She would give the hugs herself.

She sat down at her desk and turned on the machine. Her cat, Monkey Face, sat on her lap and purred.

The computer screen gave her three choices.

| RECIPES | REPORT CARDS | GORILLA ATTACK |

She moved the mouse until the curser came to the box marked **REPORT CARDS**. She clicked the button.

Monkey Face jumped off her lap, and pounced on the mouse.

"Aaahhh!" screamed Mrs. Jewls.

The cat's paws danced crazily over the keyboard as it wrestled with the mouse.

"Get down!" shouted Mrs. Jewls, as she pushed the cat off her desk and onto the floor.

The computer screen looked something like this:

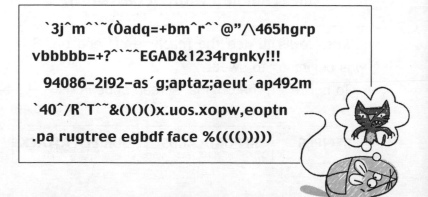

```
`3j^m^`˜(Òadq=+bm^r^`@"/\465hgrp
vbbbbb=+?^`˜^EGAD&1234rgnky!!!
  94086–2i92–as´g;aptaz;aeut´ap492m
`40^/R^T^˜&()()()x.uos.xopw,eoptn
.pa rugtree egbdf face %((((())))
```

"Uh-oh," said Mrs. Jewls.

"Okay, don't panic," she told herself. "Stay calm."

She pressed the **Escape** key.

A whole new set of strange symbols and numbers appeared on her screen.

She pressed **Back Space** but nothing happened.

She pressed **Enter**.

The screen cleared. Then a new message appeared.

> **Scrambling completed. Files cannot be unscrambled without password.**

Mrs. Jewls turned the machine off and on. She was beginning to sweat.

To her relief, the original screen appeared.

| RECIPES | REPORT CARDS | GORILLA ATTACK |

She moved the cursor to **REPORT CARDS** and clicked the mouse.

Her screen looked something like this:

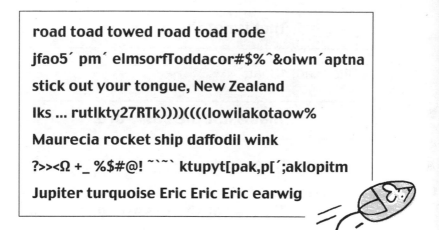

road toad towed road toad rode

jfao5´ pm´ elmsorfToddacor#$%ˆ&oiwn´aptna

stick out your tongue, New Zealand

lks ... rutlkty27RTk)))(((((lowilakotaow%

Maurecia rocket ship daffodil wink

?>><Ω +_ %$#@! ˜`˜` ktupyt[pak,p[´;aklopitm

Jupiter turquoise Eric Eric Eric earwig

Press F1 for help.

Mrs. Jewls pressed **F1** and the following message appeared.

Enter password to unscramble files.

"What password?" Mrs. Jewls asked out loud.

She typed on the keyboard. "What's the password?"

That is not the password.

"I know that's not the password," she muttered. "What is the password?"

She tried, "Apple."

> **That is not the password.**

She tried, "Boat."

> **That is not the password.**

She tried, "Password."

> **That is not the password.**

She tried, "Pig Lips."

> **That is not the password.**

She tried, "If you don't tell me the password I'm going to cry."

> **That is not the password.**

She tried, "That is not the password."

> **That is not the password.**

The report cards were due tomorrow!

There was only one thing to do. She had no choice. She had to do the report cards the old-fashioned way. By hand. She just hoped she could find all the old tests and stuff.

She jumped in her car and drove to school. She searched through her desk for her old grade book, and any old tests she could find. She dug through the drawers, the closets, and even the trash.

PROBLEM 30

Mrs. Jewls found four answer sheets from a spelling test crammed in the back of a drawer.

Jenny	Dana
1. rode	1. road
2. toad	2. rode
3. towed	3. towed
4. road	4. toad
5. rowed	5. rowed

Terrence	Stephen
1. rowed	1. rode
2. toad	2. towed
3. towed	3. toad
4. rode	4. rowed
5. road	5. road

She remembered that one of them had all five correct. Another student got all five wrong. And she knew Jenny got a better grade than Terrence.

What were the correct answers?

(**Clue** on page 98. **Hint** on page 103.)

PROBLEM 31

Mrs. Jewls found some answer sheets from a bug test on the floor of the closet.

John

1. earwig
2. octopus
3. no
4. ant
5. uncle

Joe

1. earwig
2. octopus
3. no
4. ant
5. aunt

Maurecia

1. earwig
2. spider
3. yes
4. fly
5. aunt

Joy

1. nosehair
2. spider
3. no
4. fly
5. uncle

Benjamin

1. nosehair
2. spider
3. no
4. fly
5. aunt

She remembered that John got a better grade than Joe. She also remembered that Maurecia got a better grade than Joy. And Benjamin only got two correct answers, but she didn't know which two.

What was the correct answer to each question?

(**Clue** on page 98. **Hint** on page 103.)

PROBLEM 32

In her coat pocket she found some answer sheets for a test she gave on outer space. She remembered Leslie got a better grade than Paul. Paul got a better grade than Dana. And Stephen and Calvin each got the same grade.

Leslie
1. Jupiter
2. Sun
3. Mars
4. Saturn
5. Pluto

Paul
1. Jupiter
2. Moon
3. Mars
4. Saturn
5. Pluto

Dana
1. Neptune
2. Sun
3. Mars
4. Saturn
5. Goofy

Stephen
1. Neptune
2. Sun
3. Mars
4. Saturn
5. Pluto

Calvin
1. Neptune
2. Moon
3. Milky Way
4. Earth
5. Goofy

What were the correct answers?

(**Clue** on page 98. **Hint** on page 103.)

PROBLEM 33

Mrs. Jewls had given the class a test on facial expressions. She looked through the children's desks and found the answer sheets for Jason, Bebe, Calvin, Joy, and Leslie.

Jason

1. smile
2. smile
3. rub your chin
4. puff out your cheeks
5. raise your eyebrows

Calvin

1. lick your lips
2. smile
3. rub your chin
4. puff out your cheeks
5. raise your eyebrows

Bebe

1. lick your lips
2. stick out your tongue
3. grab your ears
4. puff out your cheeks
5. open your mouth real wide

Joy

1. smile
2. smlle
3. rub your chin
4. wink
5. raise your eyebrows

Leslie

1. smile
2. stick out your tongue
3. bite your index finger
4. grab your ears
5. open your mouth real wide

Mrs. Jewls knew that Jason missed only one question, but she couldn't tell which one he missed. Somebody else answered all five questions correctly. Somebody else missed all five. One person got only one right. And she didn't have a clue about the other person.

What were the correct answers?

(**Clue** on page 99. **Hint** on page 103.)

PROBLEM 34

In the trash basket she found five answer sheets from a test on colors. Fortunately, on each answer sheet she had written how many were wrong. Unfortunately Myron's score was smudged. How many did Myron miss?

Dana *missed two*

1. pink
2. purple
3. blue
4. orange
5. yellow

D.J. *missed three*

1. red
2. black
3. white
4. green
5. brown

Dameon *missed two*

1. pink
2. black
3. purple
4. red
5. yellow

John *missed four*

1. brown
2. gray
3. blue
4. red
5. turquoise

Myron *missed*

1. brown
2. purple
3. black
4. green
5. yellow

(**Clue** on page 99. **Hint** on page 103.)

PROBLEM 35

She found four answer sheets from a test on flowers. Calvin missed two. Bebe missed two. Deedee missed four. Todd's grade was smudged. What was Todd's score?

Calvin *(minus 2)*

1. rose
2. violet
3. bluebonnet
4. pansy
5. daffodil

Bebe *(minus 2)*

1. daisy
2. petunia
3. bluebonnet
4. forget-me-not
5. chrysanthemum

Deedee *(minus 4)*

1. rose
2. petunia
3. bluebonnet
4. pansy
5. chrysanthemum

Todd

1. daisy
2. violet
3. bluebonnet
4. forget-me-not
5. chrysanthemum

(**Clue** on page 99. **Hint** on page 103.)

PROBLEM 36

Mrs. Jewls found some crumpled answer sheets stuck way at the back of her bottom drawer. They came from a test on "Nations of the World." Rondi, Allison, Stephen, and Jason missed every question. Benjamin's paper wasn't marked.

Rondi *(minus five)*

1. Greece
2. Chile
3. Iceland
4. Turkey
5. Australia

Allison *(minus five)*

1. Chile
2. Turkey
3. Iceland
4. Australia
5. Greece

Jason *(minus five)*

1. Greece
2. Chile
3. Australia
4. Iceland
5. Turkey

Stephen *(minus five)*

1. Greece
2. Australia
3. Iceland
4. Turkey
5. Chile

Mrs. Jewls remembered the questions she asked, but she didn't remember what order she asked them.

(a) What country sounds spicy?

(b) In what country would you expect to find a lot of Australians?

(c) What country sounds like a bird or a nerd?

(d) What country sounds like oily dirt?

(e) What country sounds like a great place to have an ice skating party?

Here is Benjamin's answer sheet. What was his grade?

Benjamin
1. Turkey
2. Iceland
3. Chile
4. Greece
5. Australia

(**Clue** on page 99. **Hint** on page 103.)

PROBLEM 37

Mrs. Jewls found all the answer sheets from a test on transportation. However, only four had the grades marked. Eric Fry, Eric Bacon, and Eric Ovens each got two right. Sue only got one right.

Eric Fry *(two right)*
1. rocket ship
2. airplane
3. bus
4. train
5. boat

Eric Bacon *(two right)*
1. airplane
2. boat
3. rocket ship
4. bus
5. train

Eric Ovens *(two right)*
1. boat
2. train
3. bus
4. airplane
5. rocket ship

Sue *(one right)*
1. airplane
2. train
3. bus
4. rocket ship
5. boat

Mrs. Jewls remembered the questions she asked for the test, but unfortunately, she couldn't remember the order in which she asked them.

These were the questions she asked.

(a) What form of transportation should you take, if you are in a hurry to get from Alaska to Florida?

(b) What form of transportation runs on tracks?

(c) What takes kids to school, is often yellow, and smells terrible?

(d) What form of transportation would you take to get to the moon?

(e) What form of transportation should you take to get across a lake?

Mrs. Jewls needs to figure out the order in which she asked those questions, so she could grade the rest of the class's tests. In what order were they asked?

(**Clue** on page 99. **Hint** on page 103.)

CHAPTER 12

THE NEW FLAGPOLE

The flagpole in front of Wayside School was struck by lightning.

Mrs. Jewls's class got to choose a new one.

"I think we should get a taller one this time," said Deedee. "Because our school is so tall. Next to the school, the old flagpole looked kind of puny."

"The taller the better!" agreed Ron.

"Right on!" hollered Mac.

"Hold on a second," said Eric Fry. "If we get it too tall, then the people standing at the bottom won't be able to see the flag way up on top."

"He's right," said Dana. "We can't get it too tall." Dana had trouble seeing the flag without her glasses.

"We don't need a shorter flagpole," said Sharie. "We need a bigger flag! I say we get a real tall pole, and a giant flag!"

"Oh, I don't know about that," said Stephen. "It will take a lot of work to raise a giant flag up a tall flagpole every day."

It was Stephen's job to raise the flag.

"Don't be so unpatriotic!" said Jason. "You should be willing to work hard to show you love your country."

"Let's see *you* raise the flag," said Stephen.

"I would," said Jason, "but my arm hurts from playing Nintendo."

"I agree with Stephen," said Todd. "We should get a short flagpole. That way it won't get hit by lightning again."

"Lightning never strikes the same place twice," said Deedee.

"Sometimes it does," said Todd. "I heard about a man who was struck by lightning *twice*. The first time he lived, but the second time he died. And then, fifty years later, lightning struck his tombstone."

"Yeah, but he was in a different place all three times," Deedee pointed out. "The flagpole is always in the same place."

"But it's a different flagpole," said Dameon.

"So, that doesn't make any difference," said Deedee. "Does it, Mrs. Jewls?"

"Huh?" asked Mrs. Jewls.

"If lightning doesn't strike the same place twice, which is more important: the place; or the thing being struck by it?"

"Say what?" asked Mrs. Jewls. She told everyone to write down what he or she thought would be the perfect flagpole height.

This chart shows the results.

6 Ft.	Stephen
10 Ft.	Dana
25 Ft.	Todd, Eric Fry, Allison, Rondi, Myron, Benjamin, Sue
30 Ft.	Dameon
50 Ft.	Bebe, Calvin
60 Ft.	Joe, John
65 Ft.	Kathy
75 Ft.	Sharie, Mac, Joy
80 Ft., 6 inches . .	D.J.
85 Ft.	Leslie, Paul, Eric Ovens, Terrence
91 Ft.	Eric Bacon
100 Ft.	Deedee, Ron, Jenny, Maurecia, Jason

(You will need to refer to the chart in order to answer the next 6 questions. There are no clues or hints for this set of problems.)

PROBLEM 38

Which height was chosen by the most students?

"I guess the flagpole will be 25 feet tall," said Mrs. Jewls. "Since more people chose that height than any other."

(I know. I just gave away the answer to problem 38, but it was a pretty easy question.)

"Hey that's not fair," said Jenny. " 'A hundred feet' came in second! There should be a vote between 'twenty-five feet' and 'a hundred feet.' "
"That sounds fair," agreed Mrs. Jewls.

PROBLEM 39

They voted. Each student had to vote for either "25 feet" or "100 feet."
Naturally each child voted for the number that was closer to his or her original choice. For example, Eric Bacon voted for "100 ft." because 91 is closer to 100. Stephen voted for 25 ft. because it was closer to 6 ft.

What was the outcome of the vote?

"So that will be the height of the new flagpole," said Mrs. Jewls.

"But that's not fair!" said Terrence. "Four people liked '85 feet.' We're entitled to a vote too."

"I guess you're right," said Mrs. Jewls.

PROBLEM 40

There was another vote. This time it was between "the winner of problem 39" and "85 feet." Again each child voted for the number closer to his or her original choice. What was the outcome of this vote?

"We should compromise," said Bebe and Calvin. "Fifty feet is right in the middle. If we get a fifty foot flagpole everyone will be happy."

"Let's vote," said Mrs. Jewls.

PROBLEM 41

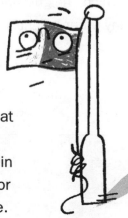

This time everyone voted for either "50 feet" or "the winner of problem 40." What was the outcome of this vote?

As you might guess, everyone in the class demanded that his or her number be given a fair chance.

So they continued having elections. It was very much like a game of tether ball at recess. After each vote, another number was given a chance to "play the winner," until at last every number was voted upon.

PROBLEM 42

In every vote, between any two heights on the chart, it turned out that one child always voted for the height that won. Who was that child?

PROBLEM 43

What will be the height of the new flagpole? (Which height wins against any other height?)

CHAPTER 13

STRANGE FACTS

(In each of the following problems you will be given a set of facts. You are to accept those facts as true, even if you think they're preposterous.

You will then be asked to come up with a conclusion based on those facts.

There are no clues or hints for this set of problems.)

PROBLEM 44

Facts:

1. All the girls in Mrs. Jewls's class like unicorns.

2. All the boys in Mrs. Jewls's class like spaghetti.

Based on those two facts, which of the following conclusions *must* be true? (There may be more than one.)

a: Jenny likes spaghetti.
b: Rondi likes unicorns.
c: Myron doesn't like unicorns.
d: Kathy hates unicorns.

PROBLEM 45

Using the same facts as in problem 44, Which of those four conclusions *must* be false? (There may be more than one.)

PROBLEM 46

Facts:

1. Dana's hair is longer than Joe's hair.

2. Joe has more hairs on his head than Dana.

3. John's hair is shorter than Joe's.

4. Dana has more hairs on her head than John.

5. All of Joe's, John's, and Dana's hairs are exactly the same thickness. In other words, if you plucked a hair from each of their heads, and cut each hair to the same length, the three hairs would all weigh the same.

(If the hairs are not cut, then one of Dana's hairs will weigh more than one of Joe's hairs because Dana's hairs are longer.)

(You might think a single hair doesn't weigh anything, but imagine if you had a million hairs piled on a scale. That would certainly weigh something. Therefore each individual hair has to have some weight to it.)

Based on those facts, which of the following conclusions *must* be true? (There may be more than one.)

a: John has more hairs than Joe.

b: Dana's hair is shorter than John's.

c: If Joe shaved his head and put all the pieces of hair in a pile, and if John shaved his head and put all the pieces in a different pile, and if Dana shaved her head and put all the pieces in a pile, Joe's pile would weigh the most.

d: If Joe shaved his head and put all the pieces of hair in a pile, and if John shaved his head and put all the pieces in a different pile, and if Dana shaved her head and put all the pieces in a pile, John's pile would weigh the least.

e: If Joe shaved his head and put all the pieces of hair in a pile, and if John shaved his head and put all the pieces in a different pile, and if Dana shaved her head and put all the pieces in a pile, Dana's pile would weigh the most.

PROBLEM 47

Using the same facts as in the last problem, which of those five conclusions *must* be false? (There may be more than one.)

PROBLEM 48

Facts:

1. Deedee cannot eat just one baloneo. After she eats one, she has to eat another. (And after she eats that one, she then has to eat another one, and after she eats that one, she has to eat another, and so on.)

2. Ron likes to play kickball after eating lunch.

3. Deedee is the only person in the school who will eat a baloneo.

4. *If* Louis, the Yard Teacher, has to mop something up during lunch, *then* nobody will get to play kickball.

5. *If* Miss Mush makes baloneos, *then* Deedee will eat one.

6. *If* anybody throws up during lunch, *then* Louis will have to mop it up right away.

7. A baloneo is similar to an Oreo cookie, except instead of the white part, there is a round hunk of baloney.

8. *If* Deedee eats five baloneos, *then* she will throw up.

9. Today at school, after they finished eating lunch, Ron played kickball and Deedee played four-square.

Based on those nine facts, which of the following conclusions *must* be true? (There may be more than one.)

a: Miss Mush did not make a big batch of baloneos for lunch.

b: Deedee threw up.

c: Baloneos taste great.

d: Deedee throws up a lot.

e: Deedee was absent.

f: Ron was absent.

g: Miss Mush shaved her head, put all the pieces of hair in a big pile, and covered it with tomato sauce.

PROBLEM 49

Facts:

1. *If* it rains in the morning, *then* Jenny will get wet on her way to school.

2. *If* Jenny gets wet on the way to school, *then* she will sneeze in class.

3. Mrs. Jewls will give a tissue to anyone who sneezes in class.

4. *If* one person sneezes in Mrs. Jewls's class, *then* at least three other children will also sneeze.

5. Jason sneezed in Mrs. Jewls's class yesterday.

Based on those facts, which of the following conclusions *must* be true? (There may be more than one.)

a: It rained yesterday morning.

b: Mrs. Jewls gave Jenny a tissue yesterday.

c: Mrs. Jewls didn't give Jenny a tissue yesterday.

d: Allison said, "God bless you, Jason."

e: Allison said, "Yuck, you're gross, Jason!"

f: Mrs. Jewls gave tissues to at least four children yesterday.

GAME DAY

On the last day of school before vacation, the children got to compete in the "Wayside Olympics." They had all kinds of races and other contests of great skill and courage.

Problems 50, 51, and 52 are based on the following set of facts. (There are no clues or hints for problems 50–52.)

1. Deedee is the fastest girl in Mrs. Jewls's class.

2. Dameon is the fastest boy in Mrs. Jewls's class.

3. The fastest runner in Mrs. Jewls's class likes to read.

4. Dameon likes to read.

5. The second fastest runner in Mrs. Jewls's class doesn't like to read.

6. The fastest runner in the class is shorter than Joe.

7. Myron is taller than Joe.

8. Dameon is taller than Myron.

PROBLEM 50
Who is the fastest runner in the class?

PROBLEM 51
Is the second fastest runner in Mrs. Jewls's class a boy or a girl?

PROBLEM 52
Who is taller, Deedee or Myron?

PROBLEM 53
THE RELAY RACE

Eight children raced in a relay race, four on each team. They were Todd, Paul, Leslie, Deedee, Joy, Maurecia, Sue, and Benjamin.

1. Leslie and Paul were on the same team.

2. Todd and Joy were on different teams.

3. Sue and Benjamin were on the same team.

4. Deedee and Todd were on different teams.

5. Benjamin and Maurecia were on different teams.

What were the two teams?

(**Clue** on page 100. **Hint** on page 103.)

PROBLEM 54
THE SACK RACE

Eight children ran in the sack race (four teams of two): Eric Fry, Eric Bacon, Eric Ovens, Terrence, Allison, Rondi, Jenny, and Sharie.

1. None of the Erics were together.

2. A team with two girls finished ahead of Eric Ovens's team.

3. Eric Bacon's team finished ahead of Terrence's team.

4. Sharie's team finished ahead of Eric Fry's team.

5. Terrence's team finished ahead of Jenny's team.

6. Jenny's team finished ahead of Allison's team.

What were the four teams, and in what order did they finish?

(**Clue** on page 100. **Hint** on page 103.)

PROBLEM 55
THE STAIRWAY RACES

There were two stairway races. In the first race, the children started at the bottom of the stairs and raced to the top. In the second race, they started at the top and raced to the bottom.

The racers were Dameon, Deedee, Ron, Allison, and Kathy.

1. The person who was the last to the top, turned out to be the winner of the race to the bottom.
2. The person who won the race to the top, came in third in the race to the bottom.
3. The person who was third to the top, was second to the bottom.
4. Kathy was fourth to the top.
5. Allison was fourth to the bottom.
6. Ron reached the top ahead of Deedee.
7. Ron reached the bottom ahead of Dameon.

For each race, tell what order the children finished.

	Race To Top		Race To Bottom
1st.	_____	1st.	_____
2nd.	_____	2nd.	_____
3rd.	_____	3rd.	_____
4th.	_____	4th.	_____
5th.	_____	5th.	_____

(**Clue** on page 100. **Hint** on page 103.)

PROBLEMS 56 AND 57
THE GREAT WATERMELON DROP

Five students were paired up with five teachers for the Great Watermelon Drop.

The five students were Myron, Dameon, D.J., Dana, and Jenny. The five teachers were Mrs. Jewls, Miss Worm, Miss Mush, Mr. Kidswatter, and Louis, the Yard Teacher.

Rules:

It worked like this:

- A watermelon was placed by a window in each classroom.

- The first student had to push the watermelon out the window on the first floor, and his or her teacher/partner had to try and catch it.

• The second student then pushed a watermelon out of the second story window, and that student's teacher/partner had to try and catch it.

• Then the third student pushed a watermelon out of the third story window, and so on.

• If all five watermelons were caught, then the student from the first floor would move up to the sixth floor, and push that watermelon out the window. And so on.

• If a teacher failed to catch a falling watermelon, then that teacher, and his or her student/ partner were OUT. But the next student still had to push the watermelon from the next highest floor. For example: If a student pushed a watermelon out the tenth story window, and the teacher missed it, they would be OUT, and the next student would push a watermelon out of the eleventh story window.

Facts:

1. All female students were partnered with male teachers.

2. D.J. went first. He pushed the watermelon out the first story window. His teacher/partner caught it.

3. The next student pushed a watermelon out the second story window. The teacher groaned as he caught it.

4. The next student pushed a watermelon out the third story window. The teacher missed it, and the crowd cheered as they watched the watermelon smash against the pavement.

5. The next two teachers caught the watermelons dropped from the fourth and fifth floor. One of those watermelons was pushed out by Myron.

6. The next two teachers caught the watermelons from the sixth and seventh floors.

7. Miss Worm fell down trying to catch the next one. The cheers were even louder this time, as the watermelon exploded on the sidewalk.

8. Jenny pushed the watermelon out the ninth story window. Her teacher caught it.

9. Mrs. Jewls caught the next one from the tenth floor.

10. *Splat!* The next teacher missed. Everyone cheered.

11. The next five watermelons were caught. Mr. Kidswatter, who was no longer in the contest, said, "Perhaps we should call it a tie. I don't want anyone to get hurt." But they decided to keep going.

12. The next watermelon was caught.

13. The student pushed the watermelon out of the window on the eighteenth floor. *Splat!* The teacher failed to catch it and the game was over.

56. Who was on the winning team?

57. What were the other teams, and on what floor were they put OUT?

(**Clue** on page 101. **Hint** on page 103.)

CONCLUSION

PROBLEM 58
EGG TOSS, SOMERSAULT RACE, AND PIE EATING CONTEST

Facts:

1. Todd signed up to be in the somersault race and the egg toss.

2. Joy would like to enter both the pie eating contest and the egg toss.

3. *If* Joy wins the pie eating contest, *then* she will not be allowed to enter the egg toss.

4. Jenny would like to enter the somersault race and the pie eating contest, but she can't because they are both at the same time. So she will enter the pie eating contest, unless she is wearing her favorite shirt with all the sparkles. If she is wearing that shirt, she will enter the somersault race instead.

5. *If* Joy enters the egg toss, *then* Todd will get egg in his hair. (If she doesn't enter the egg toss, his hair will stay clean and fresh.)

6. The only person in the whole world who can beat Joy in the pie eating contest is Jenny.

7. The only person in the whole world who can beat Todd in the somersault race is Jenny.

8. Everyone who enters the pie eating contest ends up with whipped cream on their noses.

Based on the above facts, which of the following conclusions *must* be true? (There may be more than one.)

a: If Jenny wears her sparkly shirt, Todd will win the somersault race.

b: If Jenny's shirt doesn't have sparkles, Todd won't win the somersault race.

c: If Joy wins the pie eating contest, Todd will win the somersault race.

d: If Todd has egg in his hair, Jenny will have whipped cream on her nose.

e: If Joy has whipped cream on her nose, Todd will have egg in his hair.

(There is no clue or hint for this problem.)

CLUES

In general:

Remember that in solving arithmetic problems you work from right to left. So when I speak of the "first column" I mean the "one's column," or the column furthest to the right. When I speak of the "last column" I mean the column furthest to the left.

When solving the arithmetic problems, be careful not to confuse the letter **o** with the number zero, or the letters **i** or **l** with the number one.

Some of the clues give you several steps to follow. Make sure you understand the first step, before moving on to the next one.

Problem 1:

$$
\begin{array}{r}
b\,o\,y\,s \\
+\ b\,o\,y\,s \\
\hline
s\,i\,l\,l\,y
\end{array}
$$

Notice that **b + b** has to equal a two digit number. That means that **b** has to be 5 **or more**. But the key to the problem is the circled **s**. To begin the problem, you have to figure out what number the circled **s** *must* represent. Then you will change all **s**'s to that number and solve for **y**.

Problem 2:

$$
\begin{array}{r}
g\,i\,r\,l\,s \\
+\ g\,i\,r\,l\,s \\
\hline
s\,i\,l\,l\,y
\end{array}
$$

This problem has two possible solutions.

Notice that **l + l = l** and that **i + i = i.**. They both can't be zero. What other number would cause this result? (You have to carry.) You will need to make either **i** or **l** zero. The letter you don't make zero will be that other number.

Problem 3:

$$
\begin{array}{r}
a\,r\,c\,s \\
+\ b\,r\,a\,s \\
\hline
c\,r\,a\,s\,s
\end{array}
$$

Begin by trying to figure out the letters **s** and **c**.

Problem 4:

$$
\begin{array}{r}
l\,l\,a\,m\,a \\
-\ s\,e\,a\,l \\
\hline
s\,e\,a\,l
\end{array}
$$

This is an upside-down version of the first problem. It would be the same as **seal + seal = llama**. The key, once again, is the circled **l** in llama.

Problem 5:

$$
\begin{array}{r}
l\,i\,p \\
+\ l\,i\,t \\
\hline
p\,i\,p\,e
\end{array}
$$

You should know by now that **p** has to be the number **1**. That means **i** has to be either **0** or **5**. Which one works?

Problem 6:

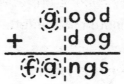

$$
\begin{array}{r}
p\,e\,p \\
+\ p\,e\,n \\
\hline
e\,r\,n\,e
\end{array}
$$

This time it should be clear that **e** has to be **1**. The key here is that **n** can't be **2**. What is **n**?

Problem 7:

$$
\begin{array}{r}
g\,o\,o\,d \\
+\ \ \ d\,o\,g \\
\hline
f\,a\,n\,g\,s
\end{array}
$$

After figuring out that **f** has to be **1**, you should be able to get **g, a,** and then most importantly **o**.

Problem 8:

```
   t o o
   t o o
   t o o
+  t o o
─────────
   h o t
```

Begin with the letter **t**. Notice that in the first column, 4 times **o** equals **t**. Therefore, **t** must be even. And if you look in the last column you see that **4** times **t** equals a single digit number.

Problem 9:

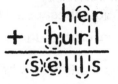

You should begin by figuring out what numbers the circled **s, h,** and most importantly **e** must be. Then notice the second column: **e + r = l**. So what is the relationship between **l** and **r**?

Problem 10:

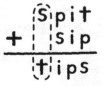

Notice that **t** is one more than **s**. That should give you **p**.

Problem 11:

$$
\begin{array}{r}
pet \\
pet \\
+\ pet \\
\hline
\text{(t)}ape
\end{array}
$$

Now that we're adding three numbers, the circled **t** can be **1** or **2**. Which is it?

Problem 12:

$$
\begin{array}{r}
yea \\
+\ yay \\
\hline
aye
\end{array}
$$

This problem was included because while making up these problems I discovered a unique quality about the number 5. Observe:

$$
\begin{array}{cc cc cc cc cc}
\text{(1)} & \text{(6)} & \text{(2)} & \text{(7)} & \text{(3)} & \text{(8)} & \text{(4)} & \text{(9)} & \text{(5)} & \text{(0)} \\
+5 & +5 & +5 & +5 & +5 & +5 & +5 & +5 & +5 & +5 \\
\hline
\text{(6)} & 1\text{(1)} & \text{(7)} & 1\text{(2)} & \text{(8)} & 1\text{(3)} & \text{(9)} & 1\text{(4)} & 1\text{(0)} & \text{(5)}
\end{array}
$$

Now see if you can find the number 5 in the problem.

Problem 13:

$$
\begin{array}{r}
still \\
stall \\
+\ stilt \\
\hline
nitwit
\end{array}
$$

In the first column notice that two **l**'s + **t** = **t** (or a number that ends in **t**.) That means that **l** + **l** is either zero or ten. The second column should answer that question.

Problem 14:

$$
\begin{array}{r}
\text{e i g h t} \\
+ \ \text{e i g h t} \\
\hline
\text{(t)a t t o o}
\end{array}
$$

Begin with the letter **t.** Don't forget there isn't an 8 anywhere in the problem. That is essential in figuring out **e** and **a.**

Problem 15:

$$
\begin{array}{r}
\text{o n e} \\
+ \ \text{o n e} \\
\hline
\text{z e r o}
\end{array}
\qquad
\begin{array}{r}
\text{t w o} \\
+ \ \text{t w o} \\
\hline
\text{n i l}
\end{array}
$$

Start with **one + one = zero.** Notice that in the first column, **e + e = o,** and in the third column, **o + o = e.** How is that possible?

Problem 16:

$$
\begin{array}{r}
\text{(M)I S S W O R M} \\
+ \ \text{Z I L L I O N(S)} \\
\hline
\text{(Z)Z Z Z Z Z Z Z}
\end{array}
$$

Start with **Z.** That should then give you the circled **M** and then the circled **S.** As you work your way through the problem you should be able to get all the letters except for the letters **N** and **R.** That is where the letter **Q** comes in. With the letter **Q** all 10 digits are used in the problem. And don't forget **Q** is more than **N.**

Problem 17:

$$\begin{array}{r} h\,i\,s\,f\,o\,o\,t \\ +\ t\,u\,t\,u\,t\,o\,o \\ \hline w\,h\,o\,k\,n\,o\,w\,s \end{array}$$

This problem also uses all ten digits. It may be helpful to write out the numbers, 0 1 2 3 4 5 6 7 8 9, and then as you figure out the letters, write the letter under the corresponding number. For example, you should figure out right away that **w = 1**. So write the letter **w** under the number **1.** As you continue to work the problem it will become useful to be able to look at your list so that you can clearly see what numbers are still available.

Problem 18:

$$\begin{array}{r} p\,e\,p\,p\,e\,r\,s \\ +\ p\,i\,g\,l\,i\,p\,s \\ \hline i\,g\,i\,v\,e\,u\,p \end{array}$$

Again it will be helpful to make a list of the numbers, even though only nine digits are used in this problem. The key to get you started is noting that in the third column, **i + e = e,** yet **i** cannot be zero, because of the last column.

94

Problem 20:

```
        m y
  X     a m
       d a y
       m y
     a w a y
```

Which letter represents the number one? Which letter is zero? Now solve for **m.**

Problem 21:

```
        o h
  X     n o
       z o o
      h o n
      h e r o
```

Notice that **o x h = o** (or a number that ends with **o.**) Also that **n x h = n** (or a number that ends with **n.**) Begin by trying to solve for **h.**

Problem 22:

Begin in the addition portion of the problem. You see that **e + e = e.** Therefore **e** has to be zero. Now look at the multiplication part of the problem. Do you see why **t x t** has to be less than ten?

Problem 23:

```
      r y e
  x     b y
  ---------
      r y e
    h a y
  ---------
    h e r e
```

Notice that **y x rye = rye.** That should give you **y.** Then notice that **b x e = y** (or a number that ends with **y.**) That should give you **b** and **e.** At first you may not know which is which, but it can be worked out.

Problem 24:

```
      d i m
  x     d a
  ---------
    m o o
    d i m
  ---------
    d e m o
```

Notice that **o + m = m.** You know by now that **o** must be zero. Now notice that **a x dim** equals a number divisible by one hundred. That means that **im** must equal either **25** or **75.**

Problem 25:

```
      s a y
  x     s i
  ---------
    n o s y
    i c y
  ---------
    a n n o y
```

96

Begin with the addition portion of the problem, and try to determine **a** and **i**. Then notice that **i** x **y** = **y** (or a number that ends with **y**.) You already know **i**. What's **y**? (It isn't zero.)

Problem 26:

$$
\begin{array}{r}
\text{r o t} \\
\times \quad \text{a t} \\
\hline
\text{r u d e} \\
\text{o u i} \quad \\
\hline
\text{e e r i e} \\
\end{array}
$$

1. Begin by determining **e** and **d** in the addition portion of the problem.

2. Notice **t** x **t** = **e** (or a number that ends with **e**.) This should give you **t**.

3. Try to figure out the letter **o** in **rot**.

4. Try to figure out **r** in the addition portion of the problem. (Notice it has to be an even number.)

Problem 27:

$$
\begin{array}{r}
\text{s h e} \\
\times \quad \text{h e} \\
\hline
\text{y e s} \\
\text{s h e} \quad \\
\hline
\text{s a s s} \\
\end{array}
$$

Notice that **e** x **e** = **s** and **e** + **e** = **s**. What are **e** and **s**?

Problem 28:

$$
\begin{array}{r}
  \text{ewe} \\
  \times \quad \text{he} \\
  \hline
  \text{yay} \\
  \text{sash} \\
  \hline
  \text{sissy}
\end{array}
$$

Begin with **y** in the addition portion of the problem. Then **e**. Then **w**.

Problem 29:

$$
\begin{array}{r}
  \text{aid} \\
  \times \quad \text{we} \\
  \hline
  \text{lied} \\
  \text{lewd} \\
  \hline
  \text{added}
\end{array}
$$

Start with the following.

1. e + d = e What is **d?**

2. e x i = e (or a number that ends in **e**) and w x i = w (or a number that ends in **w.**) What is **i?**

Problem 30 Spelling: You know that one student got every answer correct, and another student got every answer wrong. Therefore their answers must be different for every single question. Find the two students who never gave the same answer. To determine which of those two got them all right, check to see whose answers would give Jenny a better grade than Terrence.

Problem 31 Bugs: You know John got a better grade than Joe. They gave the same answer to every question, except for question 5. What does that tell you about the answer to question **5?** (You don't know yet how they did on the first four questions, just that they both did the same on them.)

Problem 32 Outer Space: Leslie got a better grade than Paul. Leslie and Paul only answered one question differently.

Problem 33 Facial Expressions: Calvin and Leslie got different answers for every question, but so did Joy and Bebe. By comparing their answers to Jason's (who you know only missed one) you will see that the person who got all five correct had to be either Calvin or Joy.

Problem 34 Colors: Dana got three right. D.J. got two right. They answered every question differently from each other. Since there were only five questions, that means that each question was answered correctly by one of them, and missed by the other.

Problem 35 Flowers: Since Bebe and Calvin each got three right, there has to be at least one question that they both answered correctly.

Problem 36 Nations of the World: To determine Benjamin's grade, you first have to determine the correct answer for each question. Notice that all four gave different answers for question **5.** Yet they all missed it. So what must be the answer to question **5?** Now move to question **2.**

Problem 37 Transportation: The three Erics each answered two questions correctly. Since there are only five questions, that means that there has to be at least one question that at least two Erics answered correctly.

There are no clues for problems 38–52.

Problem 53 Relay Race: There are four on each team. You are told that Leslie and Paul are on a team, and that Sue and Benjamin are on a team. The four of them can't be on the same team because each team has to have either Todd or Joy.

Problem 54 Sack Race: Begin by trying to figure out in what order Terrence, Jenny, Eric Bacon, and Allison finished.

Problem 55 Stairway Races: Use symbols or letters to show that the person who lost the race to the top, won the race to the bottom, etc.

Race To Top	**Race To Bottom**
1st. _____**y**_____	1st. _____**x**_____
2nd._____	2nd._____**z**_____
3rd. _____**z**_____	3rd. _____**y**_____
4th. _____	4th. _____
5th. _____**x**_____	5th. _____

This shows that some person, '**x**,' came in fifth on the way up, and first on the way down. Someone else, '**y**,' came in first on the way up, and third on the way down. And '**z**' came in third on the way up, and second on the way down. Now enter Allison and Kathy. Then try to figure out who are '**x**,' '**y**,' and '**z**.'

Problems 56 and 57 The Great Watermelon Drop: Number a sheet of paper from 1–18, each number representing a different floor. On each floor write down what happened. You have to keep track of where each team goes next. For example, the team on the first floor is also the team on the sixth floor, and the tenth floor. This gets a little tricky as teams are put OUT. The beginning of your sheet of paper might look like this.

1. D.J. and female teacher — caught

2. girl and male teacher — caught

3. OUT

4. caught (maybe Myron)

5. caught (maybe Myron)

6. D.J. and female teacher — caught

7. girl and male teacher — caught

There is no clue for problem 58.

101

HINTS

Problem 1: s = 1.

Problem 2: 1 = 0 or 9; i = 0 or 9.

Problem 3: s = 0; c = 1.

Problem 4: l = 1.

Problem 5: t = 9.

Problem 6: n = 3.

Problem 7: a = 0.

Problem 8: t = 2.

Problem 9: h = 9.

Problem 10: p = 9.

Problem 11: p = 8.

Problem 12: e = 7.

Problem 13: t = 9.

Problem 14: g = 5.

Problem 15: o = 6.

Problem 16: l = 5.

Problem 17: u = 6.

Problem 18: v = 8.

Problem 20: m = 9.

Problem 21: h = 1; o = 5.

Problem 22: t = 2.

Problem 23: b = 3.

Problem 24: a = 4.

Problem 25: y = 5.

Problem 26: r = 2.

Problem 27: s = 4.

Problem 28: y = 9.

Problem 29: i = 1.

Problem 30 Spelling: 5 is rowed.

Problem 31 Bugs: 5 is uncle.

Problem 32 Outer Space: 5 is Pluto.

Problem 33 Facial Expressions: Only one person got the correct answer for question 4.

Problem 34 Colors: 3 is blue.

Problem 35 Flowers: 3 is bluebonnet.

Problem 36 Nations of the World: 2 is Greece.

Problem 37 Transportation: 3 is bus.

There are no hints for problems 38–52.

Problem 53 Relay Race: Joy and Deedee are on the same team.

Problem 54 Sack Race: Allison's team came in last.

Problem 55 Stairway Race: Dameon won the race to the top.

Problems 56 and 57 The Great Watermelon Drop: Myron pushed the watermelon out of the fourth floor window and Miss Worm caught it.

There is no hint for problem 58.

ANSWERS

Problem 1: s = 1; o = 7; i = 3; l = 4; b = 6; y = 2.

Problem 2: s = 3; l = 0; y = 6; r = 5; i = 9; g = 1; or s = 6; l = 9; y = 2; r = 4; i = 0; g = 3.

Problem 3: c = 1; r = 4; a = 9; b = 5; s = 0.

Problem 4: m = 4; e = 6; a = 2; l = 1; s = 5.

Problem 5: t = 9; e = 0; p = 1; i = 5; l = 7.

Problem 6: p = 8; e = 1; n = 3; r = 6.

Problem 7: d = 8; o = 4; g = 9; f = 1; a = 0; n = 2; s = 7.

Problem 8: h = 9; o = 3; t = 2.

Problem 9: 1 = 6; u = 7; s = 1; h = 9; e = 0; r = 5.

Problem 10: s = 5; p = 9; i = 4; t = 6.

Problem 11: t = 2; a = 5; p = 8; e = 6.

Problem 12: a = 5; y = 2; e = 7.

Problem 13: w = 0; i = 6; n = 2; l = 5; a = 7; s = 8; t = 9.

Problem 14: a = 4; h = 6; o = 2; g = 5; t = 1; i = 0; e = 7.

Problem 15: t = 4; w = 7; i = 5; r = 8; l = 2; z = 1; o = 6; n = 9; e = 3.

Problem 16: S = 2; W = 6; I = 5; R = 7; L = 8; O = 0; N = 3; M = 9; Z = 1; Q = 4.

Problem 17: f = 0; i = 8; s = 4; h = 2; n = 7; u = 6; t = 9; w = 1; o = 5; k = 3.

Problem 18: s = 2; i = 9; l = 3; v = 8; e = 6; r = 7; p = 4; u = 1; g = 5.

Problem 20: m = 9; y = 0; w = 7; a = 1; d = 8.

Problem 21: z = 2; e = 7; n = 3; r = 8; h = 1; o = 5.

Problem 22: r = 4; i = 5; c = 7; h = 6; g = 3; e = 0; n = 1; t = 2.

Problem 23: h = 6; e = 7; a = 5; r = 2; b = 3; y = 1.

Problem 24: i = 2; d = 1; e = 7; a = 4; m = 5; o = 0.

Problem 25: s = 3; a = 1; y = 5; c = 4; o = 8; i = 9; n = 2.

Problem 26: i = 7; d = 0; e = 1; a = 3; t = 9; o = 8; u = 6; r = 2.

Problem 27: h = 1; a = 9; y = 8; e = 2; s = 4.

Problem 28: a = 6; y = 9; e = 3; w = 2; i = 7; s = 1; h = 5.

Problem 29: w = 9; a = 3; i = 1; l = 2; e = 7; d = 0.

Problem 30 Spelling: Dana's paper was correct. 1. road; 2. rode; 3. towed; 4. toad; 5. rowed.

Problem 31 Bugs: 1. earwig; 2. spider; 3. yes; 4. fly; 5. uncle.

For your information, here are the questions that were asked.

1. What is the ickiest bug?

2. What kind of bug has eight legs?

3. Can lady bugs be male?

4. Which bug can *fly*, an ant or a fly? (Hint: Look at the name of the bug!)

5. Who always wears a yellow jacket, my uncle or my aunt?

Problem 32 Outer Space: 1. Jupiter; 2. Sun; 3. Milky Way; 4. Earth; 5. Pluto.

These were the test questions.

1. What planet rhymes with stupider?

2. What gives you a *sun* tan?

3. What is the name of our galaxy? (Hint: Think candy bar.)

4. On what planet do you live?

5. What planet in our solar system is the furthest away from the sun?

Problem 33 Facial Expressions: Joy's answers were all correct. 1. smile; 2. smile; 3. rub your chin; 4. wink; 5. raise your eyebrows.

These were the test questions.

1. What should you do when you meet someone you like?

2. What should you do when you meet someone you don't like?

3. What should you do to show you are thinking?

4. What should you do to show someone you are kidding around?

5. How do you show surprise?

Despite only getting one right, Leslie still insists she answered all the questions correctly.

Problem 34 Colors: Myron missed three. The correct answers were: 1. pink; 2. black; 3. blue; 4. green; 5. yellow.

Here were the questions:

1. What's Dana's favorite color?

2. This question is written in what color ink?

3. What color are blue jeans?

4. What does g-r-e-e-n spell?

5. What is the color of my uncle's jacket?

Problem 35 Flowers: Todd got four right. The correct answers were: 1. daisy; 2. violet; 3. bluebonnet; 4. forget-me-not; 5. daffodil. However, Mrs. Jewls gave Todd, Deedee, and Bebe each an extra point because they spelled chrysanthemum correctly.

Problem 36 Nations of the World: Benjamin also missed all five. The questions were asked in the following order: bdcae.

Problem 37 Transportation: decab.

Problem 38: 25 ft.

Problem 39: 100 ft. won. (15 students voted for 100 ft. 14 students voted for 25 ft.)

Problem 40: 85 ft. won. (Twenty-four students voted for 85 ft. Five students voted for 100 ft.)

Problem 41: 50 ft. won. (15 students voted for 50 ft. 14 students voted for 85 ft.)

Problem 42: Kathy.

Problem 43: 65 ft.

Problem 44: b.

Problem 45: d.

Problem 46: d.

Problem 47: a and b are false.

Explanation for problems 46 and 47: You don't know whose hair weighs more, Joe's or Dana's. Joe has more hair, but Dana's hair is longer. However, since John has the least amount of hair, and it's also the shortest, his hair has to weigh the least.

Problem 48: a. (Miss Mush could not have made a big batch of baloneos. If she did, Deedee would have eaten them until she threw up, Louis would have had to mop it up, and Ron wouldn't have been able to play kickball.)

Problem 49: f. (You don't know for sure that Jenny sneezed. All you know is that Jason sneezed, and if one person sneezes, there's always at least three others who do.)

Problem 50: Deedee.

Problem 51: Girl.

Problem 52: Myron.

Explanation for problems 50–52: The fastest runner in the class is shorter than Joe. Since Myron is taller than Joe, and Dameon is taller than Myron, Dameon can't be the fastest runner in the class. Therefore Deedee, the fastest girl, must be faster than him. Dameon is also not the second fastest, because he likes to read, and the second fastest doesn't like to read. Since no other boy is faster than Dameon, the second fastest must be another girl.

Problem 53 Relay Race: Leslie, Paul, Maurecia, and Todd were on one team. Sue, Benjamin, Joy, and Deedee were on the other.

Problem 54 Sack Race: The teams finished in the following order:

First: Sharie and Eric Bacon; **Second:** Terrence and Eric Fry; **Third:** Jenny and Rondi; **Fourth:** Allison and Eric Ovens.

Problem 55 Stairway Races:

Race To Top	Race To Bottom
1st. Dameon	1st. Deedee
2nd. Allison	2nd. Ron
3rd. Ron	3rd. Dameon
4th. Kathy	4th. Allison
5th. Deedee	5th. Kathy

The Great Watermelon Drop

Problem 56: D.J. and Mrs. Jewls.

Problem 57: Dameon and Miss Mush were OUT on the third floor. Myron and Miss Worm were OUT on the eighth floor. Dana and Mr. Kidswatter were OUT on the eleventh floor. Jenny and Louis were OUT on the 18th floor.

Problem 58: d.

Explanation: a is false. If Jenny wears her sparkly shirt, she will enter the somersault race instead of the pie eating contest. She will win the somersault race, not Todd.

b is false. This says the same thing as "a."

c is false. If Joy wins the pie eating contest, that means Jenny must have entered the somersault race, and she will win that race, not Todd.

d is true. If Todd has egg in his hair, that means that Joy didn't win the pie eating contest. Therefore Jenny must have won it, and gotten whipped cream on her nose.

e is false. Joy will have whipped cream on her nose whether or not she wins or loses the pie eating contest.

NOTES